ABOVE & BEYOND

ANTHONY FRISINA

ABOVE & BEYOND

ANTHONY FRISINA

Photo Credits: Cover Illustration - Alen K, Angels; Inside Photos: Anthony Frisina

ISBN: 978-0-9936162-3-5

Design and Layout: VIMI Corp., Burlington, ON   www.vimi.com

THIS BOOK IS DEDICATED
TO MY MOM; ANGELA FRISINA;
WHO PASSED AWAY IN 2016.
THIS, AND EVERYTHING FORWARD
IS IN YOUR HONOUR

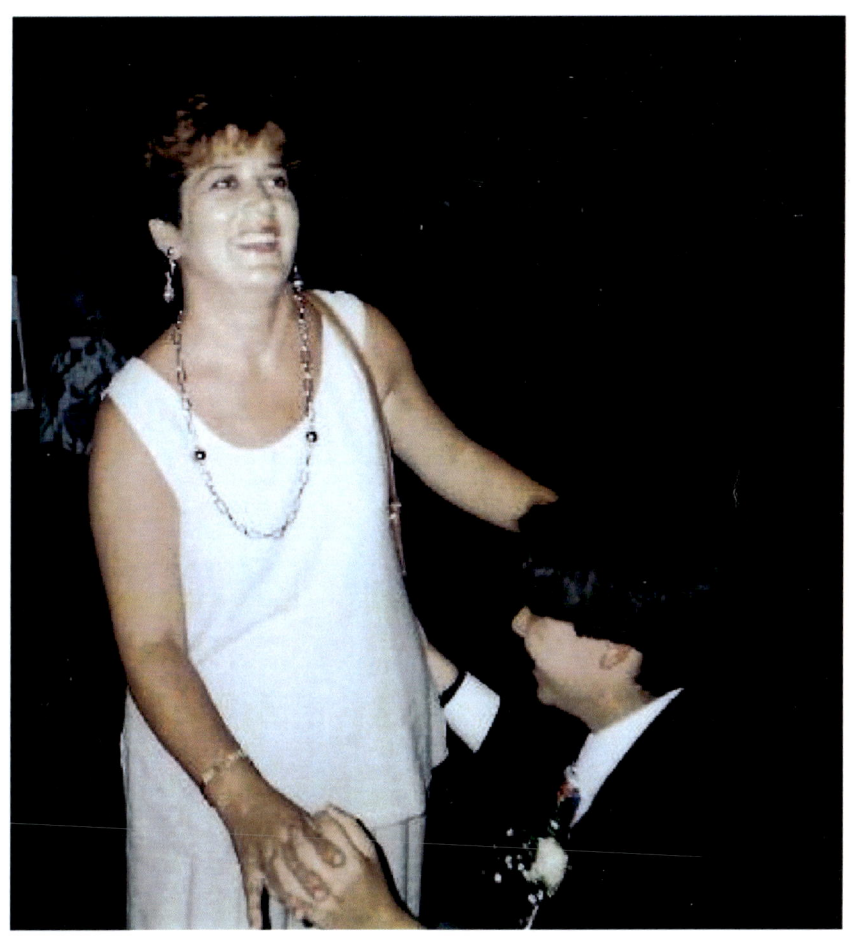

Connie Smith, Joe Frisina, Anthony Frisina

FOREWARD

Throughout more than 30 years of covering the daily news as a Canadian television journalist, I have told the stories of thousands of people from all walks of life, from celebrities to CEO's, politicians to private citizens. Reporters all want the big stories: the sensational ones like big trials, scandals, international tragedies and triumphs but in time I learned that it was the stories of ordinary people who overcome often insurmountable hardships and go on to inspire others that have such a powerfully positive impact not only on viewers but also on me as a storyteller and citizen of the world.

Anthony Frisina is one of those people. He is a change maker and has been ever since I first met him as an engaging young boy with the most beautiful big brown eyes that could melt the hardest heart. He was an ambassador for an organization that raised funds to send kids living with challenges to summer camp. Born with Spina Bifida, Anthony has turned his personal challenge into an opportunity to make change both in the way we perceive and understand disabilities and how society can and must take concrete measures to improve quality of life and everyday living.

Our paths crossed many times over the years, as he graduated from college, became an alumnus of distinction all the while advocating for the rights of individuals living with disabilities, through organizations including the Rick Hansen Foundation and the Catholic Youth Organization CYO.

A few years ago, Anthony and I discussed his concept for a television show based on his Forward Movement campaign. It was a brilliant yet daunting project but I knew with his drive, determination and commitment, not to mention those engaging big brown eyes, he could do it.... and he did it!

So here we are, a few decades later Anthony. You have now become an author, sharing your inspiring journey and creating a foundation that will carry your legacy forward for generations to come. You are helping to make this world a better place where, one day, there will be no barriers to stop anyone, regardless of their abilities from following their dreams.

Dear reader, meet Anthony Frisina. He will enrich your life.

Connie Smith, Order of Ontario
Former news anchor CHCH-TV
Conniesmith.ca
Always Good News

ACKNOWLEDGEMENTS

Being born with challenges earlier than most children, my gratitude and love goes to you, my family. My mom, my dad, brother and sister, aunts, uncles, cousins, grandparents, significant others and friends who would become family. You all showed me unconditional love; I hope that I have reciprocated that back to you. To you, my disability does not matter, I matter. Whatever the circumstances, we excelled.

Family gatherings were made special. Anthony was just Anthony and he was treated no different and that is how I prefer it. As a member of an ever-growing family, I am like many who reap the reward of togetherness. Although we may not be around the table together now as often, please know I love and appreciate all of you for your support in making me the man I am today and continue to grow to be.

To those who have supported me throughout Above & Beyond please know I am forever grateful and indebted to you for your support. Thank you especially to Lisa Narduzzi who designed the logo, Maria De Teresa, Shannon MacKinnon, Shiona Mackenzie (Ian), Cable 14 and last but not least everyone in their communities who have captured the essence of the Above & Beyond mission.

Special thanks to: MPP Monique Taylor (NDP) Thanh Campbell (Hope for the World Productions), Cody Chambers (Shop Local Perks), Max Francis (True Hamiltonian), Meghan Graham (MomentAbilty), Netasha Willis (Passionate Flashes Photography), Dylan Itzikowitz &

Jonathan Silver (The Forward Movement) and Bill King (King Asphalt Maintenance) for continually partnering with me and my work in the community.

Anthony and Family
Top Row: Joe Frisina, Angela Frisina
Bottom Row: Stephanie Frisina, Anthony Frisina,
Michael Frisina

TABLE OF CONTENTS

FOREWARD

ACKNOWLEDGEMENTS

THE ARRIVAL 1

THE ULTIMATE CONFIDENCE 5

A CHALLENGE FOR A 12 YEAR OLD 9

TRANSITION IS AN ART
    (ELEMENTARY TO HIGH SCHOOL) 13

TRUE FRIENDSHIPS 17

ADAPTIVE SPORTS 19

COLLEGE YEARS - THROUGH THE LENS OF
    DISABILITY 25

ON THE OPERATING TABLE...AGAIN! 27

EMPLOYMENT 29

ALUMNI OF DISTINCTION - 2013 33

VOLUNTEERING AND WHY I GIVE BACK 37

EDUCATING ON ATTITUDINAL BARRIERS 45

ABOVE & BEYOND: THE ORIGIN 51

MY SUPPORT AT HOME 59

A TYPICAL DAY FOR ME LOOKS LIKE THIS 61

THE 3 MONTH CURSE OF 2016 65

WHAT IS LOVE? 69

THE HAMILTON TIGER-CATS 71

PREFERRING A "DIFFERENCE OF ABILITY" 75

ON A JOURNEY OF SELF-DISCOVERY 77

CONVERSATIONS: THEN & NOW 81

TO BE CONTINUED... 83

"Birth is an opportunity to transcend. To rise above what we are accustomed to, reach deeper inside ourselves than we are familiar with, and to see not only what we are truly made of, but the strength we can access in and through birth."
- Marcie Macari

1

THE ARRIVAL

February 7th, 1980 was a day that would change the lives of Joe & Angela Frisina forever! Becoming parents for the first time. I can only imagine it would change anyone's life, let alone giving birth to a son who would face challenges earlier than most, which is another challenge in and of itself. For this part of the story you'll have to trust me as most of this is based on my memories and information from others.

Imagine; being a brand new parent who is not allowed to hold their child for long, right after birth. This was the case for my mom and dad when they were made aware that I was born with Spina Bifida AND Hydrocephalus. Immediately after birth, I was taken for emergency surgery to instill a ventriculoperi-toneal shunt, more commonly known as a VP shunt. This was just the beginning of what my infancy and toddler days would look like. I was in and out of hospital numerous times, under-going multiple surgeries because the shunt would just not operate properly. They would ultimately have to take me in to have it repaired or replaced a half dozen times. Even through all of these complications, I was loved no matter what!

Finally, it was at the age of two that my shunt would stabilize and there would be calm in our family once again. My parents knew, however, I would have to be seen regularly by what was known as the Spina Bifida Clinic – which consisted of, Neuology, Physiotherapy, Occupational Therapy, Urology and Pediatric care. I am eternally grateful to my mom for taking me to these appointments regularly and ensuring that I received adequate care.

I view every single surgery I have had in my life as a "reboot", a new beginning, a chance to take things from the past and build on them, and be a better Anthony.

I think it's important to emphasize some of the details that make me who I am. So, I will begin with some details on my surgeries, (reader discretion is advised). It was due to the level of folic acid in my mom's womb that caused me to be born with Spina Bifida & Hydrocephalus. Right after birth, I was rushed to the operating table to seize the spinal curvature and place a shunt to allow the fluid in my body to flow naturally. Being the active toddler I was, it caused me to have surgeries on the shunt multiple times; finally stabilizing at the age of 6. For years to come more surgeries were needed for tendon release, ankle fusion surgery and many shunt replacements. I am grateful to have overcome those feats as well as I have.

At the age of 8, I had a surgery that would ultimately change my life. To me, every scar signifies a battle won; making me a stronger person. It was in October of 1988, when I had surgery to release both the tendons behind my knees and a subsequent procedure to fuse my ankle bones in place, on both legs and feet. This experience led me to coin the term a "difference of ability", even though I was able to walk with the use of a cane, my posture and balance was very weak. The intent of the surgeries was to stabilize my balance and leverage my lower half, but soon another one would eventually lead me down a road from which I would never look back.

I will spare you the gory details, but the recovery from ankle surgery at 8 years old and having casts on both feet was something that temporarily gave me the feel of a wheelchair for which I would encounter later in life. Removal of the casts, was another day I'll never forget. My best friend Nick, joined my mom and I when I was getting the casts removed. I was in good spirits in spite of all that was done and what I had been through. As the doctor sawed through the cast and removed it, there was a nail sticking out of my foot, which was keeping the fusion together. The doctor had to remove a nail from each foot with a set of pliers.

Here I was an 8 year old kid with many surgeries behind me; legs in a cast below the knee with both legs taped up. I remember, having Nick by my side, as the casts were taken off, the staples had dissolved and the pins needed to be removed, I was given a sense of hope for the future. Once again, this was another victory over just another hurdle I would have to face in my young life.

A MOM'S LOVE & CARE FOR HER SON

As a young boy, my youth was challenging to say the least; surgeries, clinics, and what felt like never-ending appointments. My family was always super supportive. While my father, the breadwinner of the family, was working to provide for us financially, it was my mom who took me to all my required appointments. Visiting so many doctors, physiotherapists, neurologists, and urologists was draining which can really take its toll on anyone, let alone a young man dealing with so many health issues. Yet, it was those appointments that helped to stabilize my condition.

Sometimes the pain I feel, whether physical, mental or emotional is beyond comprehension for many people. What my mom helped me to understand is that everything I had gone through was temporary, and that I needed to find the tools to thrive. In essence, I needed to develop a coping mechanism of my own; essentially using mind over matter to alleviate the temporary measure of pain. Other tools in my proverbial tool box of survival are perseverance, resiliency, determination, faith and hope.

My mom's care for me goes above and beyond anything I would experience in my last 40 years. Mom was always there with a hug or a kick in the pants to get me back on track to reach my potential. She knew just what to do to help me to become the man she knew I was capable of being.

2

THE ULTIMATE CONFIDENCE

Another milestone came when I was 8 years old and my parents were confident enough to send me to camp on my own. Mom dropped me off in the morning at the bus pick up location where I met staff from Camp Marydale. It was great! We all took the bus together and got to know each other a little bit even before arriving at the camp. The original Camp Marydale grounds were located in Puslinch, Ontario. It's hard to believe if you know me now, but at the time I was this shy, 8-year-old out on his own for the first time on a bus heading on a 40-minute journey to what would undoubtedly change my life forever.

Here I was doing something for the first time; I was away from my parents and my school friends (they were all I had ever known up to that point). Even though I was taken out of my comfort zone, I knew I still had the support and guidance of my family. This became a special time and a place I would never forget. I met new friends; including a man with whom I am still friends. He is someone, for without him, I don't know where I would be today. It was because of John Spatazzo, I ultimately changed. It was almost immediately upon arriving when I had an epiphany! Meeting John was the most crucial meeting of my life. Meeting a man of his caliber was the first time outside of my family and core group of friends that I felt that I actually belonged in this community. His simple handshake and a welcome to Camp Marydale would change my life forever. It set me on my current path to figure out how to validate my feelings of having a special place in the World. I didn't feel like a square peg in a round hole. I was welcomed, fit in and had purpose.

Along with my one-to-one counsellors, John and the entire staff showed me how to be "Anthony, the person" rather than just some guy who uses a wheelchair at camp. They helped me develop a mindset that metaphorically my mobility aide did not exist. It was through those many conversations and experiences at camp that instilled a confidence that I still carry; in essence, the understanding that I belong. I remember going home to my parents after my first few weeks of camp and begging and pleading with them to let me go for another week; and another week after that. Two weeks lead to six weeks and to eventually the entire summer!

I was a part of Camp Marydale's one-to-one program. My years as a camper are my favourite memories as a kid. Doing group activities, such as going fishing (one of my favourite), arts and crafts, going boating or just playing catch with my one-to-one counsellors. This made me feel liberated. I was where I was meant to be right at that point in my life.

In 1993, my final year to be eligible as a camper I was given an award; they declared me the honourary camper of the year! This led to camp events and luncheons at the Royal Connaught

Hotel, meeting people like Jack Pelech, Angelo Mosca, and Rocco Romano. The many memories and takeaways from Catholic Youth Organization's Dinners, past and present are encapsulated by meeting 3 people, Lincoln Alexander, Former Lieutenant Governor David. C. Onley, and Steve Palermo, whose teachings and words inspire the work I do every day.

I was especially impacted by the late great Steve Palermo. His Major League Baseball umpiring career was cut short due to his act of heroism attempting to apprehend an assailant outside a restaurant in Texas. This resulted in him being shot in the spinal cord causing instant paralysis. He was told he would never be able to walk again. Yet, a determination and strength so strong rose up in him eventually allowing him to walk with a cane just three months after surgery. He was supported by the love and support of his wife Debbie, his family and friends through it all. He made a vow to himself and accomplished his dream to be able to walk again. As a Major League Baseball umpire he donned the number 14. After his retirement and untimely passing in 2017, no other umpire, American League, National League, or any Major League Baseball affiliations will ever wear number 14 in his honour.

Thank you Steve, for the memories and the ever-lasting encouragement to show others that to focus on your ability is what matters. Accomplishment in life lies in the strength and determination of being able to do things your way.

I didn't want to leave Camp Marydale after my tenure ended in 1993 as a camper. I made a decision, with the support of my parents, that was going to take a big leap of faith; I was

7

going to be a leader!

In 1994, I was encouraged to remain with Camp Marydale, but this time as a counsellor in training, C.I.T for short. It was a great experience and one of learning constantly. It became my responsibility to come alongside a counsellor to be a support for my younger peers. Now I got to live vicariously through them as campers, while being given a taste of leadership; something for which I passionately hold a special place in my heart. They loved the opportunity to interact with me, but most importantly, they saw me, not the wheelchair. It was a sign of the impact I was making, as well as a sign of the opportunity for future leadership roles. The 1994 season at Camp Marydale ended on another high point as I was asked to bestow the honour of representing Camp Marydale as their honourary camper for a second year in a row (the only time it was handed out twice to the same person)! I cherished it as equally as I did in 1993. It would allow me to grow and gain a confidence, that at the time I never knew existed.

With Steve's message ringing in my ears, I was not going to let my disability nor my wheelchair define me. I was going to define my path. I understood obstacles were going to be in my way and upon navigating my path, there were going to be checkpoints, some good, some not so good and many that resulted in opportunity. Someone once said, if the goal is big enough, the facts don't count. I hope that if there's one take away from reading this book, it's not the challenge that defines you, but it's how you overcome those challenges. This in part is what I believe defines character.

3

A CHALLENGE FOR A
12 YEAR OLD

At age 12, I went through a surgical experience that had the most substantial impact on my life. Some would say it was for the negative. I was walking using a cane or using a walker and crutches with different sets of leg braces prior to the surgery. Specialists had tried everything from KAFO's to AFO's and more. (KAFO is a Knee-Ankle-Foot-Orthotics and the other an Ankle-Foot-Orthotics).

The success rate in 1992 was 40%, but I felt mentally prepared for any obstacle. I had cysts beginning to form in the lower part of my spine, which is partially severed and has curvature commonly known as Scoliosis which is typical in individuals with Spina Bifida.

After surgery, I woke up groggy and popped up to a sitting position, which was not good having just come out of as serious surgery as I just did. The nurses rushed to me to make me lay me down properly so I could rest and recover properly. When I heard the news that a cyst had popped during surgery and they couldn't remove the particles that were still in me, thus rendering me unable to walk. My road of recovery to a new normal was just beginning. As difficult as it was to receive

9

this news, I was still determined to live life to the fullest. Yes things had changed radically, but I was still me, and I wasn't going to let this change my outlook on life.

With John, Nick, my friends and family by my side, I had hope for the future. I saw this as my opportunity to show the character, resilience and drive that I knew I had in me, proving something one believes starts with proving it to yourself. I challenged myself while I was in the hospital to show myself what I can do, rather than focus on what was taken away from me. It's my belief that adversity not only builds character, it reveals it.

After a few weeks in hospital at Toronto Sick Kids, they took care of the dressing on my back and worked on a mobility skillset, transitioning me into becoming a full-time wheelchair user. I started to gain the knowledge required and became more and more accustomed to my new lifestyle.

This then led me to a 3-month journey at the Hugh MacMillan Rehabilitation Centre to re-learn about life, about independence and about advocacy. I made a conscious and subconscious effort every day to grow as a person. It was an experience that if it had not have happened, I am not sure I would be where I am today on this journey through life.

THE NEW NORMAL

Returning home after my time of rehabilitation and orientation to my new way of life, I knew I would have to adapt. My living space had to change. My dad, who is not only a hard-working man, but also very handy, set his efforts to establish a space on the main floor of our home. Stairs were now my kryptonite, if you will.

My Dad added a cement ramp for accessibility to the front door. In the back of our house, we had a two-level deck, so he also built a ramp between each level so I had access to as much living space in our house as possible.

I had to move my bedroom from upstairs to the main floor while my parents and siblings still had their rooms upstairs. So we transformed the living room into a bedroom that was sectioned off by a barrier to our dining room. In time, I transferred over to the den that had a bathroom connected; so I was upgraded to a bedroom with my own ensuite bathroom, complete with a roll-in closet!

In my bedroom I had my radio, a tv, and a desk at which I was supposed to do my homework. Being a typical teenager, I liked listening to the radio, plus it helped me fall asleep as background noise. More often than not, I would get admonished from upstairs to turn the volume down. I would comply some of the time, but not always.

This new way of life did change my social life so it was imperative that my home became my Kingdom. I was comfortable and it had all of the accommodations that I required. I would hesitate going out to my friends because it was likely their house was not accessible for wheelchairs. Summertime was easier to visit because we would stay outdoors to play. Even my parents had to alter where we would go out for dinner based on the level of accessibility.

I was still being driven to school by my mom. Now, it was just a matter of transferring from my wheelchair to the front seat of our car and then back to my wheelchair once we had arrived at our destination. Funny thing, often my mom would be set to chasing after it because I'd "forget" to set my brakes before transferring. We would both have a good laugh and I would get one of her looks to do better next time.

Heading back to school was going to be interesting…

TRANSITION IS AN ART (ELEMENTARY TO HIGH SCHOOL)

My graduation from elementary school meant one door closing and another door opening. Having come back from major surgery and entering grade 7 was challenging for me personally, my family and my school. This was my first glimpse of public space accessibility and how they are built. My school had stairs galore to get to our classrooms. The elementary school preliminarily purchased a crawler which is a big machine that was attached to my wheelchair and was operated only by our custodian (maybe my best friend and a few others may have operated it a time or two, shhh). It was used to get me up and down the stairs while being able to remain in my wheelchair. It was successful for the most part. Although I learned very quickly that I had a fear of heights, it was something I needed to get over; full disclosure, I am still not over that fear!

HIGH SCHOOL DRAMA

Transitioning from grade 8 to grade 9, felt like starting all over again. Going from being at the top back down to the bottom of the totem pole. I loved grade 8. I am still great friends with most of my classmates from that year. Grade 9 came required learning how to navigate a new school and more. It made it easier that a majority of my friends from grade 8 joined me in grade 9. Through my experiences in high school, I grew up a lot.

I was a good student, not a great student, but I was dedicated to learning inside and outside the classroom. I was discovering where my passions lay. I took another leap of faith and joined the high school band and vocal ensemble after watching a performance in grade 10. It was a decision from which I would never look back or regret. I grew from the experience of being in front of a crowd, expressing a talent I didn't know I had. It was amazing to show off our talents in places like Chicago and Montreal. Going on trips without the supervision of my parents was a change not only for them, but for me as well. Looking back and knowing what my needs were then and knowing what I was challenging myself to complete on my own has made me a better man to this day.

High school wasn't all fun and games, though It was there I was introduced to de-streaming which meant for every test and every assignment there were 3 levels: basic, general and advanced. Once in grade 9, as the teacher was handing out the tests to the class when I noticed that the final page on mine was folded inward. I thought nothing of it at the time.

I completed the basic and general parts of the test, but just prior to handing it in, I unfolded the final page and noticed it was the advanced level portion. I folded it back as it was and handed it in, asking the instructor why it was folded. I am paraphrasing what she replied under her breath, "It was something you wouldn't be able to handle". (Gasp!) Even though I handed in the test, I became very disappointed in this teacher.

My mind raced, "How does one person not give people an equal opportunity based merely on mobility issues?" This part of the attitudinal barriers that I will further explain in another chapter. I spoke to many people in authority and received permission to take the advanced portion of the test at a later date. My only regret is that I didn't get to do with my classmates. Still, the important thing to me was that I was given the opportunity to complete the whole test as everyone else. A hard lesson was learned through this, but I swore to take away the positives, albeit sometimes difficult added strength in my core to counter assumptions based mindset.

"People will walk in and walk out of your life, but the one whose footstep made a long lasting impression is the one you should never allow to walk out."
- Michael Bassey Johnson

5

TRUE FRIENDSHIPS

This was an emotional chapter for me to write. I hope you can sense just how much when you read it. There is only one word to describe this chapter which is GRATITUDE. I am grateful for all that I experienced in this time of my life. From a young age, the belief that I belonged was instilled in me by my family. Yet I faced the same challenge that every kid does when making new friends. Whether it is when I changed to a new school, or faced a new social opportunity in the community, the question would plague me, was I ever going to make friends or have a best friend? So I was very grateful for the relationships I made at Little Red Apple Pre-school, and St. Agnes Elementary school, but the fact is, I still face these questions at every stage of life.

There is a photo that captures the beginning of a belief in my sense of belonging; a belief I would never ever lose. It captures a moment when I was able to walk through the library with my friend. In it, I am wearing a white sweater, blue jeans, and blue (not suede) shoes. It's a moment in time I will remember for the rest of my life.

I would continue to resonate with my peers throughout my childhood. I really can't explain why. Was it my dashing good looks or my charm? Perhaps it's the "what you see is what you

17

get" mindset. It's not out of cockiness or arrogance, but an unshakable confidence. Do those characteristics resonate with me today? I'll let you be the judge. From then on, I just knew I belonged, so the transitions of making friends, and even some best friends was seamless.

Since grade 2, when I moved from Stoney Creek to Hamilton I have been able to call one person my best friend. He knows me inside and out. He is a man of integrity and dedicated to his family and friends; the type of guy who didn't mind the occasional Taco Bell night living out our teenage angst together. We hung out with a larger group of friends. They would be on their bikes with me being pulled by bungee cords in my wheelchair. (DISCLAIMER: please don't try that at home). Fortunately, the shenanigans that most kids get into wasn't something that would bypass me. I was right in there with them, and to be honest probably instigated a few of them. (shhh...don't tell my parents)

6

ADAPTIVE SPORTS

As I got older, I learned of adaptive sports. These are sports designed to be barrier-free for persons with disabilities and include us in sports recreation like anyone else. While there are many, I was completely drawn to two of them: Challenger Baseball and Sledge Hockey (which is more commonly referred to now as Para Hockey in Canada). Again, this was just another step for me to gain a sense of confidence and belonging. Sports are a big part of my life. While I like watching them on T.V.; I was also fortunate to play on some teams that have given me great memories and life-long friendships.

Outside of the friendships made, I value the principles that were taught; working as a team, cooperation and developing a dedicated mindset paired with a competitive nature are just more tools to add in my toolbox of life.

I played for the Hamilton Sledgehammers in the positions of left wing and defence. I even had a short stint as goalie to round off my experience. Sledge Hockey (Para Hockey) allowed me to experience the game I loved watching, growing up as a young Toronto Maple Leafs fan. Participating in yearly tournaments helped me grow and gain strength in areas that I didn't know I had. I even had the opportunity to participate in the first round of training camp for Team Canada in 2003! At the very least, it was a great learning experience. During the sessions the coaches would encourage me in my strengths and provide an opportunity to get better in the areas where I needed to improve.

I remember scoring my first goal with the Sledge Hammers. It was February 4, 2001 a few days before my 21st birthday. Afterwards, my teammates congratulated me saying, "See, it's coming! Stick with it!" They encouraged me to keep doing what I was doing to the best of my abilities and my game would improve; they were right. I loved playing this game!

The other sport in which I got involved was Challenger Baseball; oh how I miss it. I retired from it in and around the same time as Para Hockey. This sport was a lot of fun. I started this prior to para hockey. For one season, my mom was actually the team's secretary/treasurer. Challenger Baseball was more of a recreation league, although we had the opportunity to travel at various times, but for the most part we resided at our home park. Teams would rotate playing each other Monday or Tuesday nights.

You'll hear me say "when you can't stand up, stand out". This proved true every time I played the game. My preferred position was first base; as a lefty it made the most sense. Yet, in the interest of fairness and team-play, we rotated positions as the coaches assigned them to us.

In the batter's box, you'll often hear the call to use your legs for power or brace yourself and drive your swing through your hips. Obviously that was thrown out the window in my case and for those who use personal mobility devices. For me, it's all in the arms; taking extremely aggressive swings which usually deterred me from having good balance. I would try to intimidate the pitcher, who was simply a member of the organization pitching to you if you chose not to use a tee. I developed a preference in who I wanted to pitch to me. I would rarely hit a "home run", but was more of a base hitter. I gained a reputation for my aggressive style of play. This included launching myself out of the wheelchair just to make it to the base if I was close enough. I was simply emulating my favourite baseball player at the time, Roberto Alomar. I never came home with a clean uniform. As soon as I got home from a game the uniform was headed straight for the laundry. More often than not our vehicle needed a little clean up from all the dirt I would accumulate throughout the game. After making this a weekly routine, I was dubbed with a nickname "Pigpen" in honour of The Peanuts character that lived within a cloud of dust; yep that was me, that's how I played.

The highlight of Challenger Baseball came in 1997. We were given the opportunity to go to Cooperstown, New York, during the Hall of Fame Weekend. It was the year when Tommy Lasorda and Phil Niekro were enshrined in the Baseball Hall of Fame. As part of the honour, our organization received the opportunity to play a game on the historic Doubleday Field, the site of the first ever Major League Baseball game! This was in addition to attending various ceremonial events. We were treated like VIP's.

So, as a young man whose confidence was growing, I felt it was my obligation to live up to the nickname of Pigpen. I had earned it north of the border and now I wanted to make an impression on those south of the border. I wanted to ensure that those who came out to Doubleday Field for this event would remember who I am and I was able to shine when the spotlight hit! First, it was by making a fantastic play while at first base. I stretched out using my push rim for support with my back wheel on the base, tagged him, and he was OUT!

Then it was my turn at bat. The anticipation of something exceptional hung in the air. Our organization knew it was coming, my teammates and opposition knew it was coming, the families in attendance supporting their son or daughter knew it was coming. My time at bat came without disap-pointment; with me trucking down the first base line, rumbling, bumbling, stumbling. Everyone saw it was going to be a close play. My moment came. I knew what I had to do to be safe at first – Pigpen, did not disappoint. Rather than do a normal belly flop, sliding into the base, my timing was just a wee bit off; resulting in a faceplant, bloodied face and damaged glasses. After the inning ended, I remembered a reporter from the local paper scurrying over to have a word with me while the game was still going on! I was back to my first base position when he asked how I was doing. I retorted "A little dirt, a little blood, that's it, I can take it!" trying to indicate to the reporter the game was still going and I was trying to give my attention to both him and the game at hand.

Picture this! The reporter was actually standing in the field of play, rather than in foul territory, which would have been far more safe. After all, I was just this 17 year old trying to play a game. It was a line drive that finally gave the reporter a little bit of a shock as the ball flew past him. Out of ignorance and fearful surprise he declared, "These kids are good!"; the parents simply nodded and agreed in unison as if to say, "of course, why would you think differently?".

After the game, in awe of what just happened, we just sat and took it all in. I actually had the opportunity to play a baseball game at Doubleday field where the first Major League Baseball game was played!

My career in para sports would end in my mid to late 20's as it was time to take that next step in life, committing to other dynamics of life, including my education, employment and volunteering.

"The future rewards those who press on. I don't have time to feel sorry for myself. I don't have time to complain. I'm going to press on."

- Barack Obama

7

COLLEGE YEARS - THROUGH THE LENS OF DISABILITY

High school taught me a lot of life skills, ones that I would take with me throughout my college life. They are both tangible and intangible and have aided me personally and professionally. Even though I knew where I was going and the path I needed to take, these skills helped my confidence in my transition to the next stage of my education. I am pleased to say that by the end of my studies as a college student, I am a successful graduate in the Enterprise Business and Office Administration - General & Executive programs from Mohawk College in Hamilton. In taking those 3 courses, I also learned valuable skills inside and outside of the classroom.

Choosing one's path in post-secondary education can be a daunting task. First, choosing the right college or university, then choosing the right program. I chose my college, not only because it was close to where I lived at the time, but also because something inside of me knew that this place someday was going to become my second home. Fast forward years later, I was right.

From 1999 to 2005 my college career was full of ups and downs academically if I am being completely honest. At times, I flourished, at other times, I struggled. On the whole, I am a student of the game of life. I value learning and personal growth, bound by the determination and resiliency to not give up.

It was those skills that landed me a job as an invigilator at Mohawk College; a person who monitors tests. I worked specifically with persons with disabilities and acted as a reader/scribe when needed. The evolution of the Testing Centre for Persons with Disabilities into the Alternative Testing Centre was a change that needed to happen. The ability to have equal access for all of our students was a step in the right direction.

8

ON THE OPERATING TABLE...AGAIN!

As significant as it was when I was 25 years old, I would like to think all 13 surgeries I had previously held significance to me. I remember the details as if it was yesterday. It was a Saturday night, I even remember that the Toronto Maple Leafs were at home to the Florida Panthers. I was watching the game in my room and my shunt had given out on me thus causing me to require immediate critical care and surgery. The time sensitivity of the surgery that was needed to repair or replace the shunt was dwindling. My parents, as strong, calm and patient as they could be, took me to get the medical help I required. I don't remember too much after the surgery.

I will never forget the experience I had while recovering in the I.C.U. Even though I was completely out of it, I had no grasp of who was around me or what was happening, I vividly remember waking up periodically and hearing sounds of crying. Imagining or assuming they were mourning the loss of a loved one, immediately I thought it might be about me; was I about to cross over to the other side? Questions plagued me like,"Was I next? What if I was?". I know, it sounds morbid, but the combination of lack of sleep and heavy doses of medication caused those feelings and queries. It happened 2-

27

3 times while I was there. From Saturday night to the following Tuesday was the longest three days of my life. As I lay there, I was forced to grapple with the meaning of life and my purpose. Even though I may not have been on the brink of death, being this close to it, I came to a real appreciation for life and all that it offers. I now realize that has made me a stronger person when facing adversity.

The recovery from a shunt revision surgery is different for me every time. This time, it wasn't until that Tuesday that I was finally able to have coherent conversations with my family, where I would not only be able to speak properly, but be able to hear and process information given to me. Finally the headaches were lessening and I was beginning to be able to move with confidence while regaining my balance, strength and power.

In all of that, finding my sense of self and personal confidence was something I missed. It's an incredibly awkward feeling losing one's self and having to regain it.

I missed school, I missed hanging out with my friends, I missed sledge hockey, but when the time was right I was able to resume my routine. It was gratifying to know that I made it through another adverse challenge and was ready for the next one when it was to come and grateful to my family and friends supporting me through another challenge.

9

EMPLOYMENT

Acquiring meaningful employment is always somewhat of a hurdle for people with disabilities due the attitudinal barriers of society and the employment community of which I also speak. Many people in a situation similar to mine, who can work and want to work are faced with an abundance of ignorance and unfounded internal beliefs. We face the stereotype of not being able to do anything for ourselves so then we find everything is decided for us without our input. It's a stigma and prevalent stereotype that we constantly have to overcome. There must be equal access and opportunity for all people to work, while having the right support in place for those with specific barriers; not as tokenism, but because it's the right thing to do. For an employer my advice is this, when you hire the right person for the job and you're able to see past the disability, there will always be a return on the investment which in turn benefits the economy and ultimately is a benefit for everyone.

My first job was as a basketball scorekeeper with the Catholic Youth Organization and the Hamilton Wentworth Catholic District School Board. It was our job as a team to work with the officials to ensure the integrity and flow of the games. It was a lot of fun and taught me discipline, dedication, and resilience in the process. I was in grade 8 at the time, I did this for the year which earned a little extra money but the intangibles for me were of even greater value.

These experiences were foundational for me in acquiring a job that I started in 2012. Even though it's very occasional, it's one I highly value and regard; that is the role of being a standardized patient. A standardized patient is someone who acts in a role to aid in students learning, whether it be by interviewing me or having them do simulated hands-on medical measures while being observed by a certified instructor.

It was a special day in 2015, when I was recruited for a role to be interviewed by students. As I entered the room the facilitator was none other than a doctor from my medical team as a kid growing up! Immediately upon seeing this man, I knew exactly who he was. (I won't mention his name, he knows who he is, and I hope he gets a chance to read this book) Here I was, so many years after he had cared for me that I was now able to enter the room as a young professional and give back to say thank you for the care provided to me at my most vulnerable stages of my life. This was the exact reason why I applied for this job in the first place.

After role-playing the interview scenario and staying in character the whole time, I immediately transitioned from the fictional character to being myself. I began to tell the class my story and disclose my previous relationship with my former doctor,the instructor. The class was completely mesmerized by seeing how a potential goal for the future would appear later in life. I have goosebumps writing and thinking about this, because I hope that one day someone reading this story believes that it could happen to them. I remain in that job today, and it's a role I cherish immensely.

Years later in 2003, I would become an administrative specialist at Mohawk College in their Student Life department. Following along the career path I had chosen back when I was a college student. While staying at Mohawk College, I would later become a technologist in an area dedicated to providing accessible and adaptable solutions for those who required it. It followed by becoming an invigilator at Mohawk College. Ironically, I remember clearly advising my parents I had just gotten the job as an invigilator and still had to explain the depths and details of the role of an invigilator to them. I was so proud of this job. It was initially designed as a testing centre specifically for persons with disabilities and evolved into the Alternative Testing Centre which encapsulated all students. It was a special day in my life for sure. The many tasks and skills acquired was no comparison to the copious amount of learning I received every day. I was diligent and dedicated to all tasks at hand. I am grateful to the people who taught me along the way in this role.

A few years later in 2011, I was accepted in a role as a Standardized Patient; a role in which I still hold today. Again, my parents, a little befuddled with the job, I explained to them the role and how it allowed me to give back in my own way, while standardized, life-experience goes a long way in the eyes of a learner.

As you can see by my patterns of work, Mohawk College has become my second home. At time of printing, my role as a

Customer Service Assistant allows me to interact with people on a daily basis; colleagues, students, and other staff. It is a great place to be. I am grateful that I was accepted in the beginning and trusted with the job I was given to do. I get to work with a great team who makes me better each and every day.

10

ALUMNI OF DISTINCTION - 2013

This night was probably the most special and most important night of my life and one I will never forget for many reasons. It really felt like a culmination of all the work I had done. It was also fuel to the fire of more work still needed to be done. It doesn't really feel like work to me, I naturally adorn this as a lifestyle. It's a way of thinking, believing as I strive to build a better community.

I knew I had been nominated by my friends at the Catholic Youth Organization. It was a weekday toward the end of May 2014, when I was just hanging around the condo when I got the call. I saw and recognized the number; it was someone from Mohawk. After I greeted the caller, they said, "Hi Anthony, it's the selection committee calling from Mohawk College. Congratulations, we'd like to welcome you into the class of 2013's, Alumni of Distinction, under the category of current employee". My heart filled as did the tears in my eyes, and I expressed my sincerest gratitude to the selection committee for this esteemed honour and vowed to live in the legacy for which the award is representative. My girlfriend was happy for me. We shared a moment in celebration together after the phone call. Immediately I called my parents to inform them of the news while still in shock with butterflies in my stomach. I remember this moment as if it was yesterday and could not believe I had been chosen.

The Awards evening not only lived up to but exceeded any and all expectations I had in my mind prior to the event. We filled two tables as so many of my family and friends wanted to be there to support me. My Mohawk College family was also there in full force. (To the tribe that joined me for this prestigious honour, thanks again for taking in this night with me). It was a fabulous dinner at Michelangelo's Banquet Centre followed by speeches from dignitaries and my fellow recipients. My intro-duction video played and then it was my moment to take the stage. My speech began with the customary intro honouring those who were in the attendance that night, I delivered my story depicting evolution, growth, experiences, trials and tribu-lations and concluded with a copious amount of thank you's to my family and friends. It was then that I was able to tell my stories of strength, adversity, perseverance and resilience. It was a mountain top experience. As I began to exit the stage, I noticed out of the corner of my eye, I was beginning to see the audience standing! I never envisioned a standing ovation, let alone, an ovation for just being me. It brought butterflies to my stomach and I had tears in my eyes.

The power of inspiration by a speaker is a culmination of how they present, with the right speed, volume, tone and body language, one can really captivate an audience. I know the word inspiration in many senses can be considered a cuss word for a person with a disability or what is more notably used in the disability community as "inspiration porn" referring to the main focus resting on the disability rather than the person's true accomplishment. I understand and I appreciate and respect how that word is overused. Many of my speeches and much of my focus is directed on my vision and mission. I am driven, passionate and dedicated to the importance of accessibility awareness and inclusion in my community! I can finally see the effect on culture change that I am having. Even though the rate of change may seem slow at times, I take pride in the evolution of the cultural change around me.

This award, while it sits proudly in my condo, is not mine alone. It belongs to everyone who has previously touched my life, currently touches my life and will touch my life in the future. The past, present and future are the 3 pillars of which the evolution of life occurs. I've learned the present doesn't exist without the past and without the present there is no future. The fact of being a community builder behooves me to acknowledge accomplishments past and present and I look forward to what the future has in store. There is immense satisfaction in the evolution of the man I have become and continually grow to be. This award is representative of everyone in the community, but also represents a desire and motivation of what's yet to be done and what will be done.

"The best way to find yourself is to lose yourself in the service of others."   *- Unknown*

11

VOLUNTEERING AND WHY I GIVE BACK

Giving back to the community is something that we should all do at some point in our lives. Whether it's short-term or something that you continue to do; for me, I find no greater satisfaction than putting a smile on someone else's face. A constant theme that you may come across as you read my stories is the importance of gratitude. It is out of a thankful heart that kindness flows. When we don't have a scarcity mindset, we are free to give to others in need.

When you are doing it without any expectation of reward; that is the true meaning of volunteering. You do this to make the difference you want to make for someone or in the community; not for personal gain. It is vital that your actions and words go hand in hand; in essence, your walk matches your talk. Through this passion in volunteering, I have met so many generous people with the same vision - when you put your heart into something and you do it selflessly, the world is a better place.

There's one organization that I would be remiss if I didn't mention – The Ron Joyce Children's Health Centre. I love giving back to the community with passion and heart to many organizations such as this one.

I remember being asked to come and volunteer at a Super-Crawl event; a massive downtown Hamilton event that is designed to bring people together. However this one was at the Ron Joyce Children's Health centre and meant specifically for kids with special needs. Happy to oblige, I was there to support our youth by playing games, engaging the kids and families while participating in activities alongside everyone. It was that night I learned that the Ron Joyce Children's Health Centre was developing a cheer squad for persons with disabilities. Mesmerized with how far we had come since I was a kid, I had to take part.

Participating with these kids is my way of acting upon the mantra of which I live; to give back and to do it selflessly. When I was asked what kind of role that I wanted to have with the kids, I chose being a cheerleader with them and It's a decision that I will never ever regret. Young or old, these kids reminded me of me when I was a kid. I am truly grateful that they took me into the group and let me learn and grow from each and every team member. I hope I have done the same for you.

THE RICK HANSEN FOUNDATION

Becoming an ambassador for The Rick Hansen Foundation was the beginning of an integral part of my life. It will always have a special place in my heart and has ignited the spark to many future initiatives of which I am currently involved. I remember Rick Hansen Foundation's – Wheels in Motion event in 2006. It was held at the Chedoke Children's Developmental Rehabilitation Program (CDRP) grounds. This event was something extraordinary for me to experience at this time in my life. The friends and relationships I formed on this day are ones that I would go on to have for a lifetime. Our goal for this event and others all across Canada is to raise funds and awareness for people living with spinal cord injuries, which is the result of a birth defect or because of an injury.

Through the efforts of a Canadian legend and hero, Rick Hansen, this dream became a reality. It started with his vision and then embarking on a 26-month journey, visiting 34 countries and traveling over 40,000 km across the world to raise awareness for this cause. To say that I have a life-long goal of meeting this man would be an understatement. For now, I stand in the shadow of this legend, while I represent the organization as an ambassador.

Upon the conclusion of the 2006 Wheels in Motion Event, I felt it was my duty to help take it to the next level. From 2007-2011 we held the prestigious event at Mohawk College in the parking lot adjacent to the residence. This event consisted of vendors showcasing accessibility and inclusion related products and services with the main event of 5 teams registering to take on everyday tasks of daily living with the added difficulty of being required to stay in the seated position of a wheelchair. For many people this is awkward and downright difficult, but then they realize they are just spending moments in this situation. Then it sinks in that for thousands of people, they will spend their whole life using a wheelchair or a mobility aide; goal accomplished. I am always hesitant to challenge my community in an event like this because I know the task is challenging to say the least, but it does provide an even deeper dive into many people's reality like mine.

For many participants it is a very humbling experience to go through. The weight of this emotion is so above what anyone could ever fathom. It's an experience that is meant for that moment, and never to be recreated again. However, I can say with 100% confidence that an event like Wheels in Motion is something participants will carry with them for the rest of their life.

I knew that planning the events from 2007-2010 would be challenging, but I wasn't stopping there. The 25th Anniversary of the beginning of Rick Hansen's Man in Motion Tour was a celebration; set up as a tribute to the living legend Rick Hansen and the work he continues to do and what I am continually inspired to do. For the 25th Anniversary there was something legendary that was going to take place. Many of Rick's ambassadors who spread Rick's message on Accessibility and Inclusion got involved. I was fortunate enough to partake in the second last leg of the day on November 11, 2011. It was a brisk fall day and I was tasked to hand off the celebratory medal to Charlie Cetinski who was selected to take it home to our end-of-day celebration at Mohawk College. Many people gathered in celebration of the progression of access and inclusion. Rick's journey and message is one that we continue years later to deliver not only by our words, but by our actions as well. It is a day that will stay with me forever, and act as a constant reminder of work that still needs to be done.

.THE DYNAMIC SYMBOL OF ACCESS

IIn 2017 I saw an Instagram post from friend and Paralympic athlete – Joel Dembe. Upon seeing this post, I was mesmerized. How could such a subtle change make such a difference? I invite you to check it out.

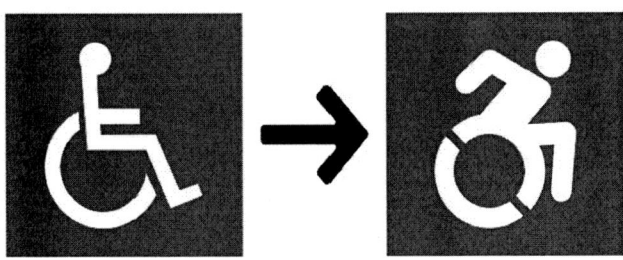

We're all accustomed to spotting the universal symbol of accessibility. It became known worldwide through Denmark by way of Sweden. The universal symbol is intended to denote ease of access for people with a disability through a building which is determined as "accessible". Recently, due to the Accessible Icon Project in the United States, the dynamic symbol evolved to the symbol on the right. It is an improved picture depicting motion and the focus is now on the human being, rather than the mobility aide. In speaking with Joel, he put me in touch with the two gentlemen that started The Forward Movement and brought this symbol and its impact to Canada. I was honoured to join their team. The symbol is now celebrated across many municipalities across Ontario, including my hometown of Hamilton.

Powerful dialogue is now starting to happen. We conduct this via intentional conversations, lectures, and guided lessons, where we share how this is more than just a symbol, it has become the catalyst for change, making it known that it's about the person rather than disability. It is significantly different from the Universal Symbol of Accessibility. The Dynamic Symbol of Access captures that people with disabilities are people first. The mission and vision to move forward on the importance of accessibility in our communities across the world must not only be heard but seen and implemented. The whole world benefits when we are accessible and inclusive for all.

Through the support and guidance of The Forward Movement, Hamilton can say with confidence the symbol resides at The Ron Joyce Children's Health Centre, The Ancaster Eye Clinic, and The Hamilton Technology Centre who took it upon themselves to create the culture change.

My favourite location that adopted this change is of course Tim Horton's Field (formerly known as Ivor Wynne Stadium), which is the home of the Hamilton Tiger Cats and the new Hamilton Forge soccer team. The day we got to install the new symbol in their parking lot was very special to me. Not only was this the second event that I had organized, but on July 12,,2018, I saw my community come together like never before. We had collaborated with the Hamilton Tiger-Cats along with the City of Hamilton. Other local community partners including the Ron Joyce Children's Health Centre and the general Hamilton community at large came out to celebrate with us. We were honoured to have MPP Monique Taylor kick off the celebration with us. This was the start of something that would ignite the fire of conversations for culture change.

Continuing the conversation is paramount, not just dialogue but one that is acted upon. Being heard must coincide with a call to action albeit a call to those in power and to those with whom you can partner to ensure the necessary changes are going to be made. As the Dali Lama has said, "Be the change you wish to see in the world". While the conversation is ongoing, we're definitely changing the culture for the better; it's vital to keep the momentum going.

"Attitude is the frame in which you view the world, the hue in which people see you, the tone in which they hear you and the mood for all your day's activities."

12

EDUCATING ON ATTITUDINAL BARRIERS

Attitudes are the eternal barrier for individuals with disabilities to thrive in the workforce is societal attitudes. We must ensure the independence, dignity and respect for everyone including individuals with disabilities, by aligning language, communication and action. This will ensure equity, diversity and inclusion in the workforce.

We may not hear someone verbally, but an action or a motion more than makes up for it. Be patient. Respect what people are saying in their own way. Communication is not always apparent via sound, but hearing someone also means focusing on them allowing their message to be sent and translated so that everyone is on the same page. As a society we must focus on all persons first and provide access to dignity and respect as well as equal opportunity.

Ableism is the preferential treatment of an able-bodied (or person without a physical disability) against a person who has an underlining disability, whether it be visible or invisible. This continues to be a barrier to accelerate to one's goals and dreams if you are a person with a disability. Overcoming that is probably one of the most challenging things we face.

Personally, I've developed a mindset that my goals, my dreams will lead to the quality of life for which I want and continue to work towards. Finding your passion is critical. When you find your passion, your work becomes your lifestyle and living a life you choose to live far supersedes the actual idea of working.

For many people however, barriers like financial support are setbacks to a quality of life that is so richly deserved by everyone. We require funding to allow us to live our lives the way we choose to, not the way society dictates to us. We must grow more to be aware of who we are as individuals and what purpose we can serve in our society. Being handcuffed to policies that at their root are designed to keep those with disabilities away from living a quality of life is reprehensible and irresponsible. We must have the power to ensure the quality of life is in our hands. The fact that finances to support quality of life for persons with disabilities aren't there or require unnecessary patience is unacceptable. There are no on-demand services for persons with disabilities. We are subject to wait times and delay, which impact the quality of lives we are entitled to live. We must face challenges of this nature with determination to be our best self. The consequences of an ableist mentality must be held accountable, but more importantly all persons must be received with respect as deserved.

Coping with the struggles of facing attitudinal and structural barriers remains a constant; we all have our ways of dealing with it. I, for one, value the challenge of overcoming an attitudinal barrier. Facing it head on with the same mindset of continually proving to myself of what I am capable of and how capable I am of doing it. This ironically is my way of shining

light on my community and those around me who sense appre-
hensions or even worse, concern. Time management is key,
proper planning is important. Living accordingly, allows me to
thrive in the paid and volunteer positions I hold past, present
and future.

Having the right supports in place and being able to overcome
attitudinal barriers, reinforces the value in you, your dignity and
ability to work. It is important for people to know that we have
the ability to create a life that we choose to live, not something
that is dictated for us.

What is the significance and why did I decide to write about
this? I believe every story should have a purpose, and bring
value to the reader. My goal is to bring awareness to prevalent
attitudes in the world. I challenge you to be mindful, aware and
understand the differences we all share, visible and invisible.
Attitudes can be stepping stones in life, and sometimes can
cause a roadblock. Hopefully, I can shed light on the power of
developing the right attitude towards people with a difference
of ability and to value who we are and what we are capable of
doing as human beings. What is the value of acceptance to
someone like me? It's priceless.

THE NEED FOR CULTURAL CHANGE

We need to change the culture. I don't tout perfection, but celebrate being a catalyst for progression, and changing culture
surrounding issues for people with disabilities. This fuels my
passion. We all have abilities, and although we may go about

tasks in a different way, we can still achieve the same outcome as our able-bodied counterparts.

We all deserve to be treated with respect and dignity, to have our independence and be in control of our own lives. We need to be our own advocate as much as possible, we must be able to have a say in how we choose to live our lives. Throughout my life I have seen a cultural shift, some good, some not so good. For the most part, our lives are becoming more and more in our control and that is thanks to various forms of funding. This enables us to hire the service workers we need and set the schedules around when we need the assistance.

Due to the rate of change in technology and the ability to work and learn at a distance, even the workplace environment has changed and created more accommodations to hire people with disabilities. More and more people are being encouraged to work remotely allowing people with disabilities to stay in the comfort of their own home. Yet there is still a long road to change the attitude of employers to be as equally confident in hiring people with a disability.

For me, culture change really advanced with my introduction to the Dynamic Symbol of Access. The evolution to the dynamic symbol is a good example of the need for change. It opened up a conversation that was often overlooked and over-shadowed by assumptive mindsets. This change is starting to move the needle from the idea that the parameters of disability should be dictated for us, to the parameters being dictated by us.

I see now that education is growing around the concept of accessibility awareness and inclusion. We must protect our independence and ensure the quality of life for persons with disabilities as it is for all persons. Issues of inclusion matter today and in the future like never before. It is and always will be an uphill climb; momentum is key. We must keep the uphill climb moving forward and ensure that we are treating everyone equally. It is imperative that we become allies, supporting the community in times of need. Bridge building shows that we all belong, and everyone deserves to have control of the life they want to lead.

*"If you believe in a dream and
have the courage to try,
anything is possible."*
- Rick Hansen

13

ABOVE & BEYOND: THE ORIGIN

In 2017, I found myself at the right place and the right time. It was just after my mom had passed. I needed something positive to happen, and it did! An instructor whom I have known for years during my continued tenure at Mohawk College, advised me of Cable 14 and their initiatives to involve the community. I had known about the station and its programs in the past but really didn't think too much of it to be completely honest. It was only after a friend decided it was her time to pitch a show and was awarded a season that I too decided it was time to take my passion, my mission and vision to the community. Thank you to my friend Maria, for showing, guiding and believing in me enough to come alongside me as I created not only a show, but now I was focused on re-energizing the community on accessibility awareness and inclusion. This was my gateway to making a difference in the community.

Following my passions for accessibility awareness and inclusion, I decided to establish Above & Beyond. It is not just a show on local cable, but it's my platform to connect with my community. I take the opportunity to engage with the public through speaking at motivational community events, partner

51

with businesses and local influencers for the purpose of moving the agenda of accessibility and inclusion forward through discussion. Through demonstrating the power of lived experiences, conquering adversity and living out a passion with a goal of alleviating assumptions-based mindsets, I am proving that including people like me makes the world a better place.

The show has undergone various incarnations. Starting with a pilot, we were then awarded 6 episodes of which I sat behind the camera and produced. I was then given a second season where I produced and co-hosted with my great friend and former support person, Shannon. I am forever indebted to those who guided this rookie on the ins and outs of creating a show beginning to end. I am committed to be a life-long learner in all areas of my life and meeting so many wonderful people throughout this process I became a sponge, ready and willing to soak up as much information as possible. Through 2 seasons, the message has become clear- People First.

From now on, if I have anything to say about it, it is that people with a difference of ability are never going to be considered as afterthoughts. While it remains an on-going battle, we, as people with disabilities, remain the largest minority group and deserve to be heard and represented accordingly. Progression is something that I am committed to. I don't tout perfection, but I do celebrate the progress that has been made. From what I can tell the response has been nothing but positive and we continue to march on to our collective goals.

Only by building alliances will our community grow stronger together in this area of beating societal perceptions and overcoming attitudinal barriers. We are raising our voices to be heard in an effort to call to action those in power to hear and act upon the changes that must be made. By collaborating with those who garner the same mission and vision, we will see a day when we can choose to live life without restraints or barriers. That, my friends, is inclusion. Inclusion is simple in theory, but rarely practiced. Progress is the key because perfection is a pipedream. If we ever attain perfection, for what then do we have left to strive? Perfection leaves us with nowhere to go, in some sense we remain at a standstill.

Life ought to be a journey of becoming the ideal version of you; while peeling off the layers and becoming vulnerable in order to attain the truth; as tough as some truth is to face. When dreams are fulfilled and passions are followed, life becomes worth living.

Above & Beyond has become my lifestyle and my passion. I strive to assure everyone is treated with respect and dignity all the time. The key principles I have developed from various speaking engagements are shortened to the acronym M.I.I.C.E.E. (Motivation – Inspiration - Innovation – Celebration – Education and Empowerment. We need to have conversations that reinforce the importance of removing attitudinal barriers and amplify education on inclusion and equality. It is the soft skills of respect and dignity that are of the utmost importance to youth. This is why the M.I.I.C.E.E. principles matter to me so much.

When we live out of assumption, we tend to neglect people. When we merely react, it's often out of panic. Yet, when we engage with all parties involved, we create a bright new future. By involving the community that will be directly impacted by a decision, we are making progress in bridging the gap of an "us and them" mindset. When people act on assumption, they make "make due" decisions and are only making more work for themselves in the long run. Basing our decision on mere stats falls short. Numbers are important, but they only tell one side of the story. There are many stories that need to be heard in our community. We all have an incredible story to tell. Isn't it time we expand the vision and allow all stories to be told? This is my platform to tell my story and a platform on which I invite others to tell to engage with me. This is the gateway to collective prosperity.

IT'S YOUR WORLD...I'M JUST VISITING

From time to time this thought crosses my mind. The world can be an interesting place, although I will admit from the mid 80's to now there has been some definite improvements, but there's still a lot of work to be done. Please note that for the purpose of this discussion, when I say "we", I am referring to us who have a difference of ability. I firmly believe that the barriers that we face make us stronger, whether you have a difference of ability or not. It's the barriers that are put on "us" from society that need improvement. How can society be called inclusive when all of it is not accessible? Please humour me, as I indulge you with some of my insights. Hopefully, if you ponder, ingest and analyze it as I have, you'll begin to take notice of the discrepancies.

While the built environment is something that I pay extra attention to, I've certainly become aware and privy to those tangible barriers that don't often get acknowledged unless we ourselves, or we know someone are directly impacted by it. Here are some questions we face:

- Why can't we access a building independently?
- Why isn't signage readily available and in alternative formats
- Why is the washroom not accessible?
- Why isn't there access to braille or extra large fonts for those who have visual impairments?
- Why aren't there audible sounds installed such as beacon?
- Why can we not access the same entrance, rather than having to go out back or go left and there's a ramp?
- Why must we ask for assistance for an everyday task that is second nature to our able-bodied counter-part, that if the right supports were in place, we could do ourselves.

The answer is simple. It comes down to money! Basically, the return on investment for many business owners or organizations doesn't appear to mesh well with the company's bottom line, thus rendering those with disabilities the inability to provide them with a business transaction.

Why doesn't the government see a return on investment? A question that still stumps me to this date. Societal barriers need to be in mainstream discussions and moreover be moved to a call to action. Being proactive, rather than reactive is the approach I always recommend when doing site assessments and participating in meetings. I must reinforce a quote from earlier, "in life, there are no problems, only unfound solutions". When taking on issues from a problem-solving mindset during times of anxiety or adversity, rather than exerting our energies toward the solution, we only exacerbate the problem and procrastinate. Then we end up creating more work for ourselves. More often than not, simplicity is the way to go.

Why don't we take the time to get it correct at the outset rather than be forced to retrofit something into a smaller space simply to comply with the Ontario Building Code? Our goals ought to be aimed at exceeding that. In the employment industry we have quotas, we have standards, we have deadlines. Shouldn't we consider this when striving to be fully inclusive? The cost of building accessible from the beginning is an added 1% rather than retrofitting an existing building, which costs substantially more. Our building environments need to be able to include everyone, no matter what.

Now, let me be clear, when I refer to the word "build" in this case, I am not referring to just the physical nature of a structure. We need to build a society where we can all be free to participate in recreation, live freely, and find meaningful work – This constitutes quality of life, inclusion for all and collective prosperity.

For example, we should have open access to public and para transportation to live with dignity and respect. More affordable housing, transitions in income to support the changing societies and the way people live. Let's create a society where there is no judgement, only encouragement to be the best version of ourselves. We often take our abilities for granted and overlook those whose abilities may be considered different thus not recognizing the support needed for all persons to ensure quality of life, dignity and respect .

"Caring has the gift of making the ordinary special."

- George R. Bach

14

MY SUPPORT AT HOME

In 2012, I made the leap of moving out on my own, much to my parents' chagrin. Something that should have happened in 2011, but after several attempts to apply for funding, I was denied on multiple occasions and offered the opportunity to go through an arbitrary process, after spending nearly a year of completing paperwork and making numerous phone calls. The reason I was denied: my situation of living at home with my parents in a safe environment did not warrant me any funding for support to make my new home accessible. At the time of appealing decision after decision, it crossed my mind briefly, "am I doing too much?" "Why am I being penalized for living in a healthy environment? I mean, I deserve support too right?" For weeks, that haunted me. With the support of my parents, we finally found the perfect space and made the decision to transform the condo that I currently have into a fully accessible space specifically designed for my personal accessibility requirements. I made sure I was a part of the process every step of the way. Finally it was moving day and I moved into the condo. It was close to my parents and where I work which for the most part made the decision one of the easiest and best decisions I have ever made. Prior to moving in, I began doing my research for options for support available to me through many organizations in the community. Ones that would assist me in my daily routine and activities. I needed to learn and look and find support to be as independent as possible; understanding my parents weren't going to be available 24/7. There is great support for those who qualify. It was time for me to look for additional help and this is where I learned about direct funding.

Direct Funding (also referred to as Passport funding) is a specialized aid available for those who need it and qualify for the program. The process was rigorous and tedious, to say the least. I started the process before I moved out; filling out paperwork, answering questionnaires, sitting on waiting lists and doing interviews based on my specific needs. Once I was accepted into the program, all the pieces fell into place. This funding goes to support my basic needs, the hiring of a bookkeeper and taking on a responsibility of hiring someone to help assist with daily tasks I struggle to do on my own. I wanted to take this opportunity to hire people that were learning as I too was learning, so I felt that this type of person would be the best match for me. I have seen many come, learn, grow with me, and go on to be the wonderful people they are in the professional world. I am truly grateful for the support personnel who have been there for me; however, there is one person that has come and unfortunately gone. Her name is Shannon. Shannon is a constant giver, a healer, and an amazing supporter. She is a true lover of acting and the arts. She also lives out of a dedication to serve the community in her own special way.

15

A TYPICAL DAY FOR ME LOOKS LIKE THIS

Writing this chapter was an interesting exercise and liberating to say the least. I thought it would also be beneficial for others to learn what "a day in the life of Anthony" looks like because like many persons who use mobility aids or have a disability, it is different than what is most commonly understood. Please keep in mind, each person with a difference of ability has a different lifestyle and different abilities, but here's mine. A character trait I probably got more from my mom than my dad, is getting up early. When I was living with them, it would be approximately 6 AM or so on a regular basis; depending on the day and what I had to do.

Today, my wake-up call is usually around 5am. I have set my alarm for that time. Although, it's usually the cat's yearning for breakfast that wakes me up more often than not. Depending on the day's schedule ahead of me, I usually try to do as much pre-planning the night before, just to be prepared as much as possible.

More often than not, I tend to wake up after what amounts to approximately 3 hours of decent sleep and more hours of broken sleep during the night as I tend to toss and turn. I find if I keep my radio on for a little white noise, it helps settle me for the evening.

Waking up at 5am is somewhat also a comfort for me and allows me to take my time. Like many other people, I am set in my ways and find that sticking to routine usually dictates the tone for the day. Being a morning person, I try to prioritize my day with completing the most important stuff and proceeding from there.

My typical day starts with breakfast, fruit and a coffee (small, one milk if you're offering to buy me a coffee one day). I'll then prepare the cat's breakfast and drop it off on my way to the lavatory. Mentioning pre-planning for the following day, I typically have my clothes for the day on hooks accessible to me in the bathroom. You also need to remember my condo is completely modified for the life of a person who uses a wheelchair like I do. I go to brush my teeth, floss, and prepare for my shower. Unlike most people, I can roll into my shower and easily transfer to a seat in the stall. Properly doing transfers and my way, everything is executed to the best of my abilities with no glitches. I am prepared, however for everything, thanks to the support(s) I have in place.

Like most people, I put on my pants one leg at a time, but the caveat for me is that I have to sit on the ground. I have all my toiletries and necessities for getting ready located at a lowered level which makes for easy access. Then I lift myself from the ground to the wheelchair after getting ready. It's also important to note, for me, that I need to have my shoes on for most activities. This gives me the stability and traction needed to counter with my upper body predominately, which takes the brunt of all my transfers. Depending on the day, whether I am spending it at home or going to work, I make sure I have paratransit pre-booked if needed.

As my day continues on, whether I am coming back home or already at home, I reflect on the day so far. Then I prepare dinner; if I am lucky it is already made for me. After dinner, I like to settle in for the evening. Don't get me wrong, I am not opposed to a night out or anything, but if I am working, building community or out at an event with friends, I prefer to remain low-key. I'll often have a support worker here to assist me with required tasks then I'll check in with family and usually call it a night early in the evening.

Wherever I am, whatever I am doing, you will see me in the best of spirits, proud that I am able to do all that I do with this community behind me. Whether I am working or volunteering, I am living my best life and the way I choose to live until societies comply on a full-time basis supporting inclusion as mainstream.

*"Grief does not change you,
Hazel. It reveals you."*
- John Green

16

THE 3 MONTH CURSE OF 2016

This is probably the most difficult chapter to write and to talk about. I'll try to put it into words, but will probably not do it justice. I know it's a part of life and that eventually we have to go through this experience at one point or another, but it doesn't make it any easier when you're in it. The pain that I have endured the first 40 years of my life, mentally, physically and emotionally, is incomparable to the loss of a loved one so close to you; one who undoubtedly made the most impact in your life in ways no one could ever imagine.

I'll never forget the car ride home on June 9th, 2016. I was supporting my friend Shannon at one of her stellar perform-ances. My parents had graciously offered to pick me up after the show. The car ride home was quiet and somber, so I knew something was up, but I wasn't going to be the one to break the proverbial ice. As we got close to my condo, my mom said in a very weak voice, "so... they found something in my stomach". I looked at my dad who was driving, and he didn't seem like himself, so I knew deep down something bigger wasn't being said. I was conflicted, I didn't want to mention anything, but I wanted to be encouraging. As we pulled into my parking lot, I proclaimed to the back seat where my mom was sitting, in my strong, powerful voice, "Mom, whatever it is, you're tough, you can take it, and kick it's ass!"

While trying to settle in that night, I found I was emotionally and physically exhausted from the events of that evening. Getting ready for bed was a struggle. I remember having constant chills and butterflies come over me. For the next few weeks, things were normal and it was mom doing her thing; picking me up for work or taking me where I needed to go that day. Then suddenly that just stopped. Mom needed to take care of things for herself, with my dad's help of course. It was then that I transitioned to an even greater need for independence. Sure, there was the support of my extended family for which I am eternally grateful, but I needed to do more things on my own; I had to find another "normal" for me.

As my mom's condition worsened, we were privy to gaining more information in that she had the C-word: lung cancer. My dad was a hero, driving her to all her appointments and consultations, but you could see her weakness loom larger as the days passed. Our family made it a point to spend as much time as we could together. Weekends were spent lounging around, just laughing and enjoying each other's company, till one day, my mom had a hospital stay at the Juravinski Cancer Centre.

Through her faith of God and her own internal strength she pulled through and was deemed fit to return home. However, her condition would never improve, she stabilized for a while until she digressed again on September 8, 2016. I received a call from my brother early that evening stating that we had to go to the hospital since things were not looking good for Mom. In layman's terms, her insides had burst and toxins from the cancer were taking over her body. The doctor suggested surgery was a possibility, but it was very unlikely she would even make it past the anesthetic. Surrounded by family, my mom laid in her bed and we took turns sharing stories of our times together; time passed with some laughs and some tears. Mom asked to meet with her immediate family individually. As the painful reality would start to set in that she was no longer with us, she set out some strict guidelines for us to follow and to know she would be watching over us. Each conversation ended with - "I love you."

I had gone home September 9th early in the morning, and arrived only to receive a phone call telling me of her passing. I was back at the hospital within the hour and sat by her side. The sights I witnessed that day, I wish upon no one.

While I can't speak for the others, I have tried to live my life according to the guidelines that she had set out. I can say without a shadow of a doubt that while I haven't been perfect, I have been persistent. As a matter of fact, this writing is in her honour; rest in paradise mom.

Having the plethora of surgeries myself and undergoing the adversities I have endured, there is nothing that will ever compare to the pain of losing my mom. She was my support line for 36 years. When I needed her; she was there, no questions asked. From being my ride, to being there for me at all times of the night because I was sick to just being someone who would not simply listen to me but hear me; that meant more than anything. There's no greater bond than a mom and her son. She's with me now writing this and I thank her for her support from afar each and every day.

My new normal began a few days after processing what had just happened. My life would move on in its own new way, I knew everything I was going to do from that point on would be in her honour. From the beginning was a matter of literally just finding myself again. While going back to work, after a 3-day bereavement leave, I couldn't believe the support I received from my work family. For that, I am eternally grateful. I had a tough time getting back and processing information. It would require a lot more training to get back what I subconsciously lost in my head. When routine is taken away from me, my ability to adapt to a new routine is probably one of the toughest things for me to go through.

As the days go by the pain of losing her doesn't go away, I have just learned various coping strategies. One of those ways is through what I do in the community, by volunteering; giving back is for her. Since she gave so much to me and to so many people around her, I knew I needed to pay it forward in my own way. She's looking down on me right now and I know she is proud of me.

17

WHAT IS LOVE?

This chapter heading ends with a question mark on purpose. Love means many things to different people, young or old. For example, the love of a family is different from the love of a significant other. Romantic love is something even more rare and something I thought would be unachievable for someone like me. For years it was, but at the age of 31 years old, my life changed. I actually met someone, who saw beyond the wheelchair and saw me; for that I am forever grateful. She taught me so much about myself. When I was with her, the fact I was in a wheelchair didn't matter. It simply remained a vehicle to my freedom and liberation. I am grateful for our relationship and the steps along this journey we took together.

Eventually, I would move onto another relationship and meet some incredibly special people who came into my life, quite honestly, at the right time. I am grateful as I grow and learn through each relationship; grateful for the way each one has impacted me in ways that I never thought possible. Only by going through this experience did I learn in ways that words can't express. It really opened my eyes to something I ultimately thought was impossible, and yet it was made possible.

It was through a dating website that I met my first girlfriend. I enlisted the support of very special people in my life who helped me express in words that would best capture who I am for whom my profile was meant. Putting yourself out there is a vulnerable experience and can be intimidating; especially for someone who uses a wheelchair as their personal mobility device. I chose to describe myself in a certain way and share that I don't believe I am defined by a mobility device alone. The culture of love and my perspective on dating continues to change from my own personal lens of experience, and seemingly through the lens of others I have dated.

I would go on to meet others on these websites who also saw and accepted me for me. It was almost surreal to also feel the same way as the others and treat me as if the wheelchair was non-existent. It was refreshing to share this feeling of mutual respect and understanding for who we were as people. I don't know why this should surprise me so much, but I catch myself sometimes looking back fondly and think, was this really real? As many relationships go, we would have moments of awe and wonderment about each other, but eventually decide that remaining friends was the path that was best for us.

I have had the privilege to love and be loved. Thankfully, I continue to meet people that hold special places in my heart. Love in its true form is one of the most powerful feelings one can share with someone else.

18

THE HAMILTON TIGER-CATS

I've got a few great stories in relation to my hometown team, the Hamilton Tiger Cats (Ti-Cats), that relates to the message of inclusion. The Ti-Cats have ALWAYS been an important part of my life. As a young six year old I remember watching games on TV with my dad. I have so many memories of getting together and being in awe of players like Earl Winfield, Mike Kerrigan, Tony Champion, and the list goes on from yesteryear to the current roster. It's awesome to see a team that continues the tradition of building community.

My dad took me to my first game when I was 6 years old. We ventured to the friendly confines of Ivor Wynne Stadium (now Tim Horton's Field). At that time I could walk, albeit short distances. While sitting there on the cold bleachers, I was in awe. My dad wanted to make sure I was having a good time. It was a great experience for me! At one part of the game, I remember my dad asking me if I was hungry. I was, so he got us each a hot dog and handed me some ketchup packets. As I was unwrapping the hot dog from the foil my dad asked if he could help me with. On the one hand, there was six-year old Anthony who was empowered and determined to do it himself, and on the other hand there was a side of me that would be glad to accept the help. At this juncture, this little Anthony decided not to accept the help of his dad (gulp).

To make a long story short, ketchup ended up going everywhere; and miraculously, some even managed to get on the hot dog. Most of it however, ended up landing in the hair of the lady that sat in front of us. My father looked at me incredulously. Now the debate was on; should we tell her or should we keep it to ourselves and hope no one else notices? We mutually decided to keep it to ourselves. Later on in the game the score was close. The climax of the game came during a potentially costly turnover and the lady in front of us (also a passionate and dedicated Ticats fan), clasped her hands on her head in despair and simultaneously ran her fingers through it. Then after seeing her hands, she panicked. You could see the expression in her body language - where, what, how did this happen? At that moment she didn't know what it was or what was on her hands? Fearing the worst, she looked to her husband and remarkably her husband remained calm as a cucumber. He also seemed to be unsure of what it was. Upon the nervousness and trepidation, the paramedics alongside her husband calmed her down, ensuring her it was ketchup.

My second year as a season ticket holder was a time I'll never forget based on how the season started. Tiger-cats headquarters located then on Jarvis Street was having a street party for the fans and introducing the team. I'll never forget one player who made his way to me as I sat in awe of what I was experiencing during the street party. "Hi, my name is Peter Dyakowski," he said and extended his hand out to shake mine.

Funny how the smallest and kindest gestures can amount to the biggest impact.

Another momentous event that sealed the deal for me however, was at my 7th birthday party when my father persuaded the player the one and only Grover Covington, to attend my birthday party! Unbeknown to any of us that his invitation was accepted and I was elated when he arrived. It was my favourite birthday ever! There was a magician and on top of that, Grover Covington making this kid smile from ear to ear. That's when I truly realized the Hamilton Tiger-Cats were more than just about sports, but embodied the love for this community it is ingrained in its team spirit.

As a season ticket holder for many years I've made a lot of friends. We all have the common bond of being loyal Tiger-Cats fans. Another amazing experience came five years later when we, as true fans, made the trip to Toronto to cheer on our team in the Eastern Final. Even though I was going solo I knew I was going to make friends along the way so that was not a big issue for me. I had to be in a separate car on the train because the dedicated section for Ticats Fans was not wheelchair accessible. Even so, many fans were scattered throughout the train and so along the way I had many conversations that were positive and enthusiastic. We arrived in Toronto and went to a pre-game party at Jack Astor's Restaurant. Unfortunately, once again the facility was not very wheelchair friendly and in order to access the floor on which the party was, there was a set of stairs and no other way up. Yet, Tiger-Cats fans, being as loyal and as awesome as we are, there were two gentlemen who offered, "we'll help you up, but we'll be too drunk to get you down". So I had the option to go up or stay downstairs; of course I took them up on their offer. Jason and his cousin assisted me up the stairs and we partied, and partied hard. How did I get down to go to the game? I'm actually not 100% sure. I am fairly certain that it was by the help of Pigskin Pete (our team's resident superfan) who assisted me down. To top it off, it was a great game, which we won!

You will find me at Tim Hortons Field alongside my heroes, Jason et al, come say hi! We are always at the top of section 102 cheering on our team.

ROUND 1 PICK 5

CFL DRAFT

TIGER-CATS FOOTBALL

ANTHONY FRISINA

K | MOHAWK COLLEGE

PRESENTED BY
FirstOntario
CREDIT UNION

19

PREFERRING A "DIFFERENCE OF ABILITY"

Changing people's perspective on disability issues has become something that I deal with in my day to day life. It's not easy changing perspectives, In fact, it's darn near impossible. It's not easy creating a paradigm shift that is so entrenched in people's psyche. Of course, my own personal perspectives are always evolving by keeping an open mind and hearing other people's perspectives. It's a matter of being able to adapt without sacrificing your morals; it's always a delicate balance. I would like to say that I have seen it all, but I anticipate being surprised in the years to come. I have gone from the viewpoint where I was born just to exist with an upheaval of ambition only to flatline where in this world I am told too, to a greater purpose of what I proclaim in my lifestyle to make an impact.

When someone asks about my disability, I will subtly correct them before answering and suggest, "a difference of ability". It creates a pause and gets the other person thinking and to acknowledge the difference between the statements. Although we achieve the same goal as the person intended before the conversation started, that subtle change puts us on a new path of respect and equity along the journey. It's a simple change to make, but makes a big difference to me, the person being addressed. A polite but frank statement opens people's minds to equality, and moves the subconscious thought, "can he do something?", to rather "how is he going to do it?". The answer will always be, in my own unique way, and that needs to be seen as ok. I have developed a "can do" attitude. The fact is that my difference of ability just makes me achieve the same task in a different way than most.

In saying "a difference of ability" is in no way shape or form a means of deflecting or deeming the word "disability" as a bad word, but merely to focus on the ability of doing things my way. Finding an atypical solution leads me to a great sense of accomplishment and allows me the gratification and satisfaction in accomplishing the goal. A quote that I live by is In life there are no problems, only unfound solutions. We need to find what is our best solution to be our best self. I focus my strengths and positive attitudes towards a difference of ability as my approach to making an impact for myself. If others see it, that is great. How it impacts others, that remains to be seen.

20

ON A JOURNEY OF SELF-DISCOVERY

I am continuously on a journey of self-discovery as I have grown up and aged from boy to man. What is normal? Is it the way I do something in comparison to my able-bodied friends that makes me "ab-normal"? Is how I conduct my everyday life and activities of daily living unorthodox, assisted or unassisted?

This was something to me, that I have been able to conceptualize into the word "Normal". Finding your own way is your normal. It's ok for everyone's normal to be different. I suggest that you don't deviate from the person you are. I've learned to just live and that asking for help is okay. I've realized that being the keeper of my own life is important. Take my advice, own your life - take the bull by the horns and show yourself what you can do. It takes heart, courage, and may even mean escaping your own comfort zone at times. The community will take notice and only then, in my opinion, will people take notice of you. Before, there is the perception in the belief of what you're unable to do, this will allow them to trust in your abilities and what you can do.

Having a mindset of continuous self-discovery keeps me going. It is something that is important in my life and about which I am very passionate. The greatest thing in self-discovery is sometimes as you live your life, a new discovery is made without you even being aware of it. Hindsight is 20/20 because reflecting back on it and seeing the difference makes it that much more special. Even as a child, I learned I was capable of doing things for myself. For instance, learning to tie my shoes was different from my friends. Some people bend at the knee, others use a step, but for me I learned that it was best to sit on the floor as we would recite the bunny ears song.

Yield to the words of the great Frank Sinatra and Do it your way! We've only got one life to live, one life to enjoy. So use it as an opportunity to impact future generations for the good and you'll never regret it. For me that's the impact that I am choosing to make. On your path of self-discovery, take note and notice everything, even the little things. Whether you see it right away or at some point down the line you'll be surprised at what you learn consciously and subconsciously. Every discovery made will influence future discoveries and opportunities.

MANAGING EXPECTATIONS

I love my community in Hamilton, Ontario, a city marveled with opportunity. People with a difference of ability are often faced with the stereotype and stigma of disability. Subconsciously, I used to and sometimes still approach social situations with the question of, "how will we be received?". Growing up, I wasn't sure how my world around me would react to me based on disability, but thankfully my parents instilled in me the mindset to approach my fears straight on. So now I visualize showing people what I can do and see myself being accepted for being true to myself. I do this for no one else's benefit other than my own; otherwise, I would be a shut-in, assuming no one would accept me the way I am. I can't force people to like me, but I have to leave it up to individuals to choose how they want to relate with me. Acceptance comes in tangible and intangible ways; meaning people will outright show me they accept me and want to tell the rest of the group, while others will just treat me like anyone else in the room. See the difference? It's simply about showing and acting out of respect.

Even though I am a professional and motivational speaker, at times I have to let my actions speak louder than my words. To me, an action towards equity versus a word or two about equity better represents the value of what a person holds in contribution. I challenge everyone to be more self-aware and present when around persons with disabilities, whether it's day to day or if it's more on an occasional basis.

Often in our initial interaction with people, we will speculate and assume we know the situation, but the truth is that we are more often than not aware of the true challenges people face on a daily basis. Treating others with respect includes, when approaching someone with a difference of ability directly or through an advocate, make sure you ask rather than assume the person needs assistance.

As a person with a disability, being in control of your own life, or, as an advocate of the life of a person with a disability can be challenging. So don't let others manipulate, advise, perceive, or judge what someone can and cannot do, whether it's you or someone for whom you're an advocate. Allow one's own voice to be heard and present, to determine what is right for them. It's time that we as a community appreciate that in order to be a unified front, we need to simply unite on the value of mutual respect that we should have for one another.

21

CONVERSATIONS: THEN & NOW

I am often faced with this head on from the community, whether it's intentional or not. It's somewhat of a challenge to discuss and I am sure it will be met with some challenging points of view and perspectives. I welcome and appreciate them. For the purpose of this book, I will share my own perspectives and mine alone. I was faced with this dilemma while hosting a Rick Hansen Wheels in Motion event on June 13th, 2007 at Mohawk College. I found myself happily bombarded with a lot to do along with my team and the City of Hamilton representatives. We had to make sure things would run as smoothly as possible and fortunately, they did.

In the spur of the moment, something changed, while subtle in nature, it was significant for me. I was asked by a local media representative for an interview; I was shocked even to be asked, (not so much anymore). Without thinking, I immediately accepted the offer. Before the interview began, the interviewer asked me probably the toughest question I could ever imagine. It was something that definitely got the hamster wheel turning, and still something that I think about to this day. My response hasn't changed. Trepidatiously the interviewer asked how he should position and present himself; should he stand or sit?

Are we to go side by side or in front of one another? The interviewer was adamant in making sure there were no inconveniences to me. However, in doing so, I became flustered. I thought to myself, aren't we just supposed to act natural around one another? For me, the more one tries to make me feel comfortable especially during a conversation, the more uncomfortable I feel. Here is some food for thought to help process this, I repeat, perfection is a pipedream so let's just celebrate progression. When approaching me, don't make assumptions, it's better to use consideration and dialogue to find a mutually agreeable solution. I don't like being pandered to, but the reality is that accommodations will likely need to be made. I'm ok with that, as long as I'm not made to feel like I am an inconvenience, otherwise I am a pretty easy going person. Language is great and this man's courtesy in asking was the right thing to do, but at the same time as we converse with one another we educate, we ensure that we people are treated as people first.

One more quick story that I want to share and still happens to this date, is that, and let's use a restaurant for example, I come in, whether with friends or family, that I am often subjected to others answering that I can answer, "What's on the menu? What would "he" like to order? Everyone started looking at me wide-eyed, my friends knew I could answer myself, my family knew as well. Being sometimes exposed to this is dehumanizing. This is why we need to ensure we have the proper support in place, educating on inclusion, making sure we don't assume anything, be mindful and patient without passing judgement. Who knows you might be surprised.

22

TO BE CONTINUED…

My story isn't over. In fact, it's just beginning! I have so much gratitude to my family and friends that have supported me along the way; I thank you from the bottom of my heart. My passion is fueled with love and passion for this community. If there is one thing that I would like all of you to take from reading my story, is the simple message that we all belong. We must treat each other equally and with respect and dignity. Our personal circumstances should not dictate the treatment of one another person, because as we all know, circumstances change, but words can cause eternal wounds. Let's give each other the same opportunity to love and be loved, listened to, heard as well as understood and most of all to be included.

Throughout all the trials and tribulations I have learned that our voice is our most powerful weapon in our arsenal that we possess, if we use it properly. A voice is more than a composition of words, sentences, and paragraphs expressed vocally. It's more than just what you hear or see in print. A voice is your business card to show those around you in the community that you are present. It entitles you to the right to belong. The right to find the inner strength and courage to have your say

Life is a journey. There is so much more to come and I plan on taking full advantage of the opportunities that come my way. I see it as a chance to prove to myself, and show that I am enough. We need to demonstrate that change is in the air and we deserve our rightful place at the table for discussion. I have learned to be resilient, apply ingenuity, and see the big picture. I expect life to be a rollercoaster of emotions, filled with fears and then an abundance of gratitude and eventually at the end of it all a sense of relief. I want to make sure I look back and have no regrets, only fond memories. I want my legacy to live on and grow in those whom I've touched and inspired. There is still a lot of work ahead of me to do, I look forward to the adventure that awaits! This is created for all of us to unite together, this is how change happens, you are welcome to join me...

ABOUT THE AUTHOR...

Anthony Frisina was born and raised in Hamilton to parents Joe & Angela Frisina and is the eldest of 3 siblings. He has a brother Michael and a sister Stephanie.

Born with Spina Bifida and Hydrocephalus his infancy was challenging to say the very least. Having been faced with many adversities in his youth, he chose to attack it with a head-on approach and let the cards fall where they may.

Mentored by many influential people along his journey, Anthony has now chosen to give back in his own way. Above & Beyond is more than just a brand, it's a lifestyle. As a social influencer, he is a speaker who is driven to empower others to collectively bring about accessibility and inclusion. His mission is about progression, not perfection.

He is working to build the momentum to ensure this conversation is included in everyday life, not as an afterthought. He envisions a day that our youth aspire to ensure that everyone belongs and that everyone is treated equally. His desire is to abolish ableism once and for all by leading the way in his community toward a much needed fundamental, systemic and cultural change that will benefit everyone. He is not daunted by this task and confidently works to bring people's attitudes in alignment with his vision for a better world for all.

Anthony lives to MOTIVATE, INSPIRE, INNOVATE, CELEBRATE, EDUCATE and EMPOWER through word and deed.

To contact: www.anthonyfrisina.ca or e-mail info@anthonyfrisina.ca

"The only way to shape your future is to discover who you are today. Without knowing your current reality you can't create your future reality."
- Unknown

BRIDGING THE GAP TO ACCESSIBILITY AND INCLUSION

ANTHONY FRISINA
ORDER OF HAMILTON RECIPIENT
2020

CHAPTER 1 - THE ARRIVAL

"Birth is an opportunity to transcend. To rise above what we are accustomed to, reach deeper inside ourselves than we are familiar with, and to see not only what we are truly made of, but the strength we can access in and through birth." - Marcie Macari

CHAPTER 2 - THE ULTIMATE CONFIDENCE

"When I was a child my mother said to me, 'If you become a soldier, you'll be a general. If you become a monk, you'll be the pope.' Instead I became a painter and wound up as Picasso." - Pablo Picasso

CHAPTER 3 - A CHALLENGE FOR A 12 YEAR OLD

"The future rewards those who press on. I don't have time to feel sorry for myself. I don't have time to complain. I'm going to press on."
- Barack Obama

CHAPTER 4 - TRANSITION IS AN ART (ELEMENTARY TO HIGH SCHOOL)

"We don't stop going to school when we graduate." – Carol Burnett

CHAPTER 5 - TRUE FRIENDSHIPS

"People will walk in and walk out of your life, but the one whose footstep made a long lasting impression is the one you should never allow to walk out." - Michael Bassey Johnson

CHAPTER 6 - ADAPTIVE SPORTS

"You miss 100% of the shots you don't take" - Wayne Gretzky

CHAPTER 7 - COLLEGE YEARS THROUGH THE LENS OF DISABILITY

"Adversity not only builds it reveals it" - Unknown

CHAPTER 8 - ON THE OPERATING TABLE...AGAIN!

"It's not stress that kills us, it is our reaction to it." — Hans Selye

CHAPTER 9 - EMPLOYMENT

"There is no greater disability in society, than the inability to see the person as more" - Robert M. Hensel

CHAPTER 10 - ALUMNI OF DISTINCTION - 2013

"You measure the size of the accomplishment by the obstacles you had to overcome to reach your goals." - Booker T. Washington

CHAPTER 11 - VOLUNTEERING AND WHY I GIVE BACK

"The best way to find yourself is to lose yourself in the service of others." - Unknown

CHAPTER 12 - EDUCATING ON ATTITUDINAL BARRIERS

"Attitude is the frame in which you view the world, the hue in which people see you, the tone in which they hear you and the mood for all your day's activities."

CHAPTER 13 - ABOVE & BEYOND: THE ORIGIN

"If you believe in a dream and have the courage to try, anything is possible." - Rick Hansen

CHAPTER 14 - MY SUPPORT AT HOME

"Caring has the gift of making the ordinary special." – George R. Bach

CHAPTER 15 - A TYPICAL DAY FOR ME LOOKS LIKE THIS

"I try to live my life every day in the present, and try not to turn a blind eye to injustice and need." - Susan Sarandon

CHAPTER 16 - THE 3 MONTH CURSE OF 2016

"Grief does not change you, Hazel. It reveals you." — John Green

CHAPTER 17 - WHAT IS LOVE?

"Love may not make the world go round, but I must admit it makes the ride worthwhile" - Unknown

CHAPTER 18 - THE HAMILTON TIGER-CATS

I thought about the problems I had growing up: how I prioritised football over school, but people were telling me I wouldn't make it, that it wasn't possible. The thing is, I did make it, thanks to my own will and determination and the help of some people I had around me in my hometown. - Richarlison de Andrade

CHAPTER 19 - PREFERRING A "DIFFERENCE OF ABILITY"

"You couldn't relive your life, skipping the awful parts, without losing what made it worthwhile." - Unknown

CHAPTER 20 - ON A JOURNEY OF SELF-DISCOVERY...

"The only way to shape your future is to discover who you are today. Without knowing your current reality you can't create your future reality." - Unknown

CHAPTER 21 - CONVERSATIONS: THEN & NOW

"One good conversation can shift the direction of change forever" - Linda Lambert

CHAPTER 22 - TO BE CONTINUED...

"Life is a journey that must be traveled no matter how bad the roads and accommodations." – Oliver Goldsmith